Dogs Fun Color

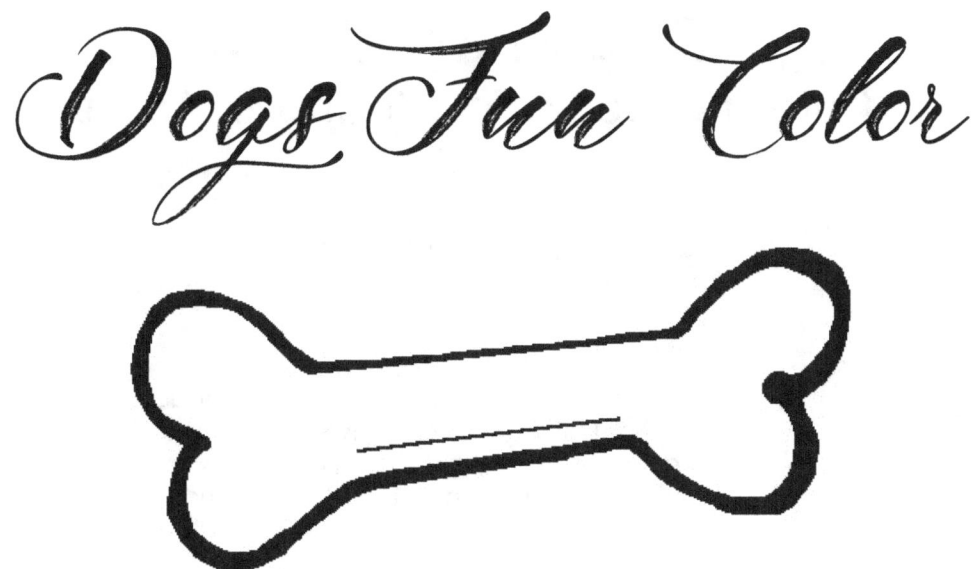

Coloring Book For Young & Adults

Bobby Lucy

Dogs Fun Color
Coloring Book For Young & Adults

Author: Bobby Lucy

Printed In The United States Of America
1st printing May 2018

ISBN: [1720459355]
ISBN-13: [978 1720459354]

Dogs Fun Color
Coloring Book For Young & Adults

Introduction

Suitable for ages 6 to adult, "Dogs Fun Color" is an inspiring and fun language used coloring book for adults that contains 30 classic colorable images for your enjoyment. Colorable text titles are included.

Coloring for adults can be very therapeutic, and is a relaxing and fun pastime for many!
The idea behind this unique book is to spur your fun creative side while producing enjoyment, stress relief, and relaxation.

There are no 'wrong' color choices and the choices are yours to make to create your own unique interpretation of the 30 images that follow.

Try to think of funny languages that dogs speak in new ways as you journey through your coloring adventure. Take your time and let the fun of adult coloring smooth your day to day stresses.

Grab a cup of your favorite beverage, curl up in your favorite quiet corner, and turn the page to your next exciting coloring subject to understand more about dogs. From tears to laughter, Dogs Fun Color has it all covered.

Enjoy!

"If you want to conquer the anxiety of life, live in the moment, live in the breath"
~Amit Ray, Om Chanting & Meditation

DEDICATION

SPECIALLY FOR MY LOST DOG "BOBBY" IN THE YEAR 1993. AND TO MY CARING PARENTS IVY LOW AND AH SENG. AND ALSO, MY RESPONSIBLE SIBLINGS LOUIS NG AND JUSLINDA. AND TO MY NIECES YUERONG AND SERVONNE AND NEPHEW HONGYI. AND MY LOVELY IN-LAWS LIM AND SUHUA.

ACKNOWLEDGMENTS

"I was very happy with the experience I got from Dogs Fun Color in the way it is not only entertaining but affordable!" – Adams Tree

"It is very creative in its words, I enjoyed the humor very much! Thanks, Dogs Fun Color..." – Michelle Lam

"The coloring book is very up to modern expectations in the way that it suits many of us, especially in the way we react to things, patience and speed has it all covered, very good job!" – Dennis Joe

ABOUT THE AUTHOR

The author is born in Singapore who had won a first place in ARTS during her high school in Tanglin Secondary School in 1996. She is now 36 belonging to horoscope DOG.

She used to own a dog in the past and the dog went missing somedays. She misses it and decided to write a book for it.

She enjoys her free time doing Arts like making cards, bookmarks, booklets and coloring. She does not hide from coloring as she thinks it is helpful in training up one's patience and multi-tasking ability.

She encourages the mentally weak to pick up coloring as a hobby as it proves to be useful in times of boredom and healing effects to the brain is very much worthwhile to own a coloring book from Dogs Fun Color.

Dogs are known to be honest and friendly animals to own in a family. It proves to be a stress reducer hobby and a good security weapon.

Many people own dogs to treat them as house guards and even several others treat dogs as close friends.

So bond your feelings today with Dogs Fun Color and have an enjoyable fruitful time!

YES?

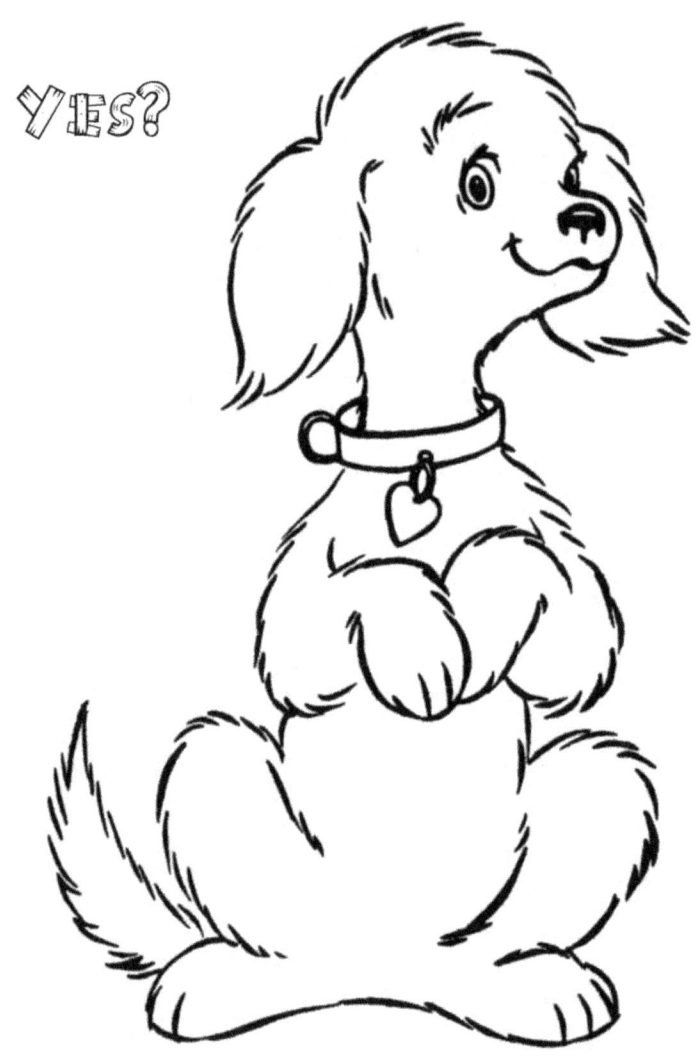

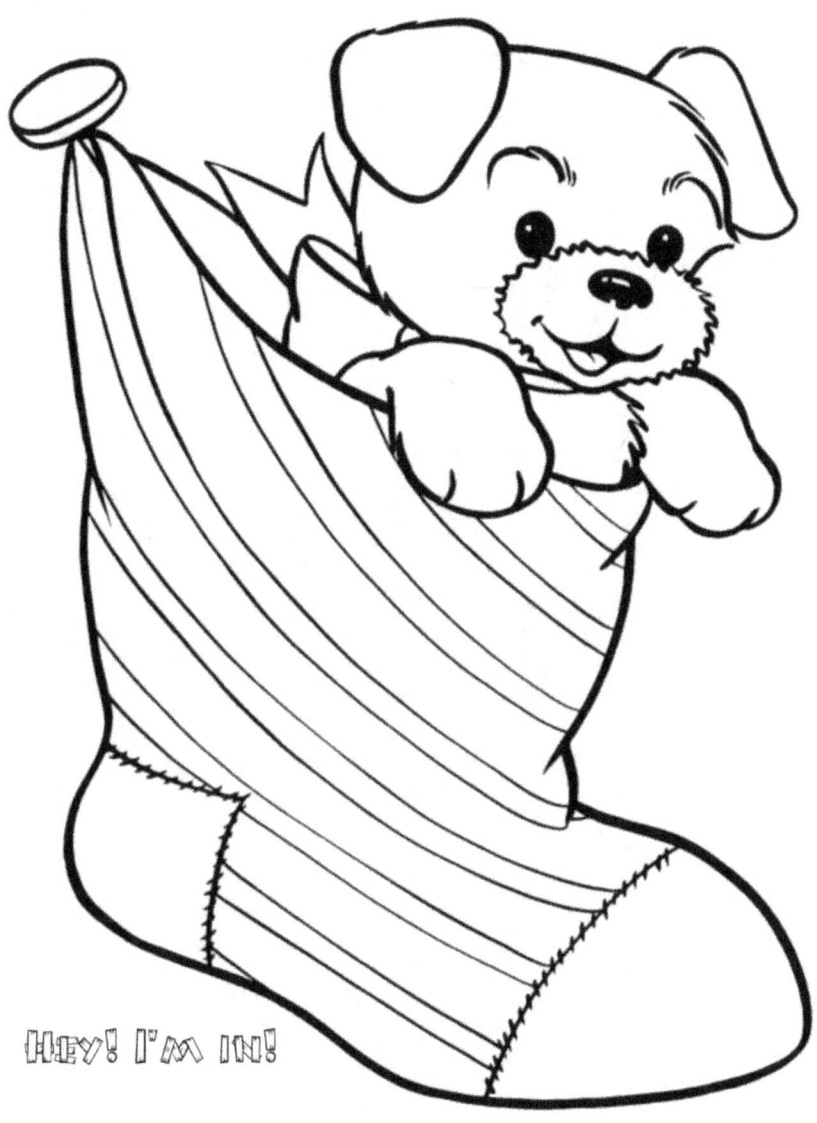

HEY! I'M IN!

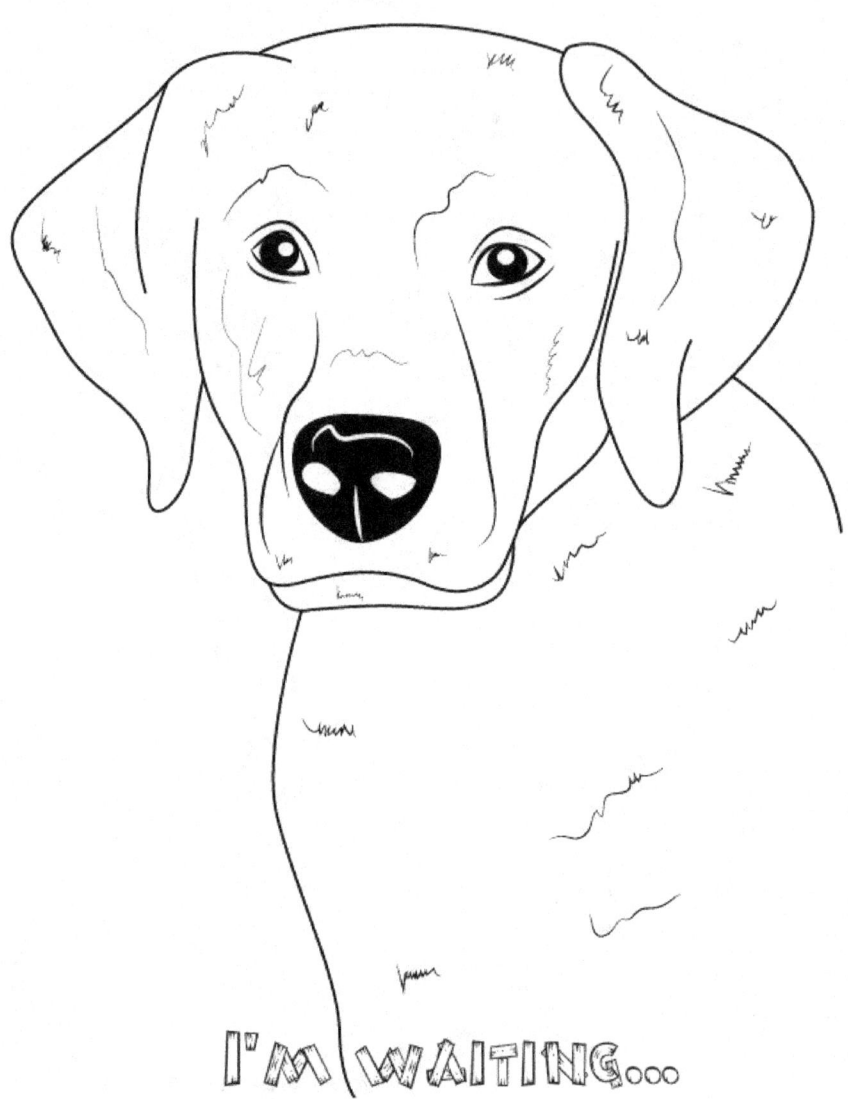

I'M WAITING...

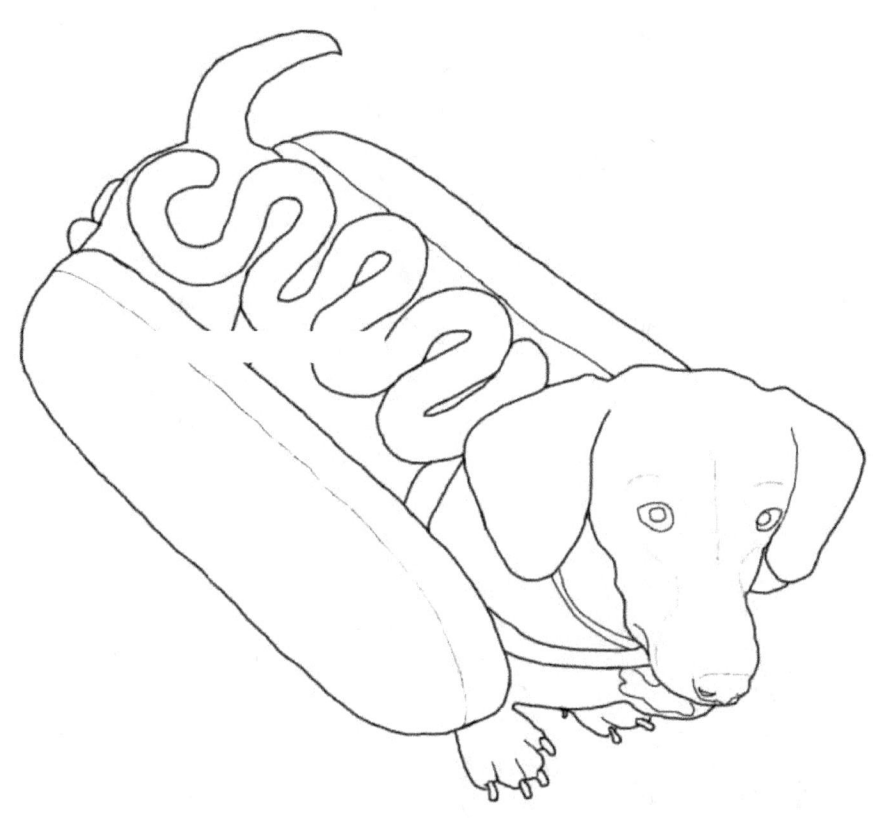

HOTDOG OR SWIMMING?

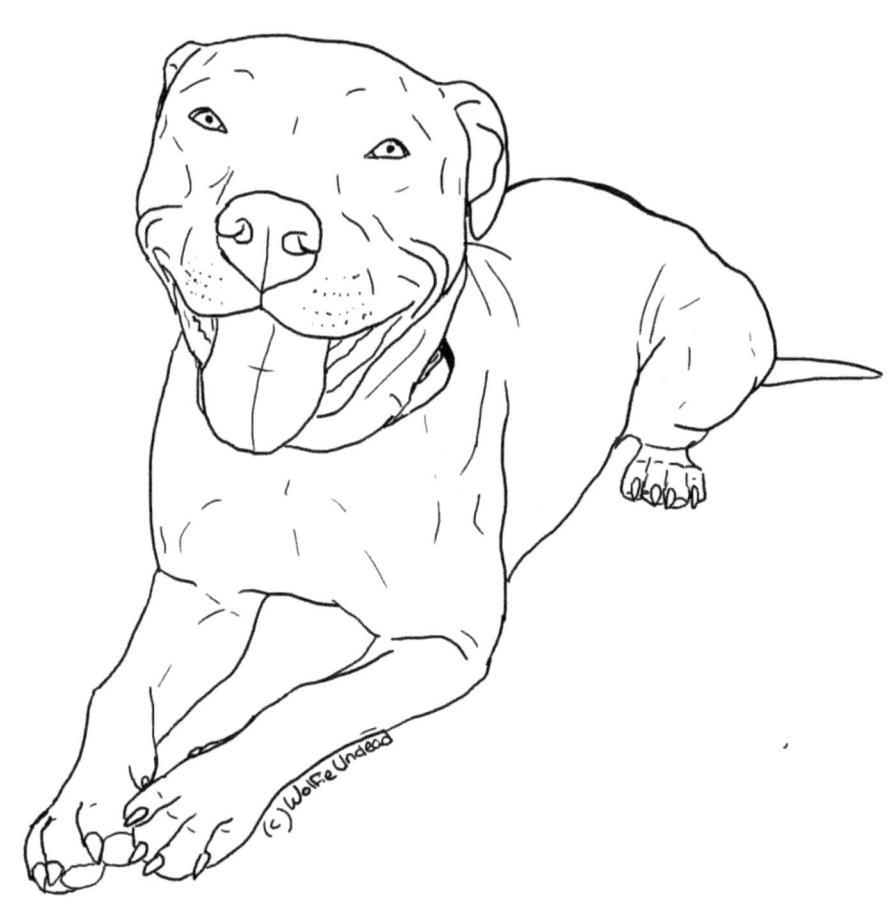

After a day's out.

LOOKING FORWARD TO FUTURE.

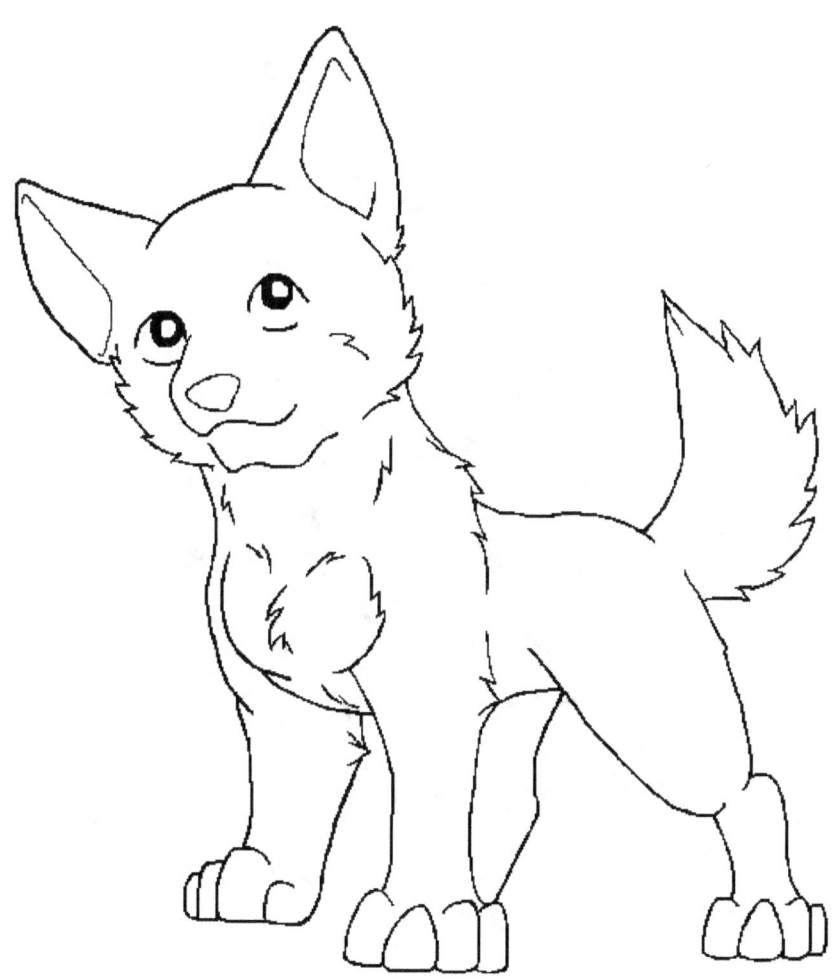

WHERE HAVE YOU BEEN?

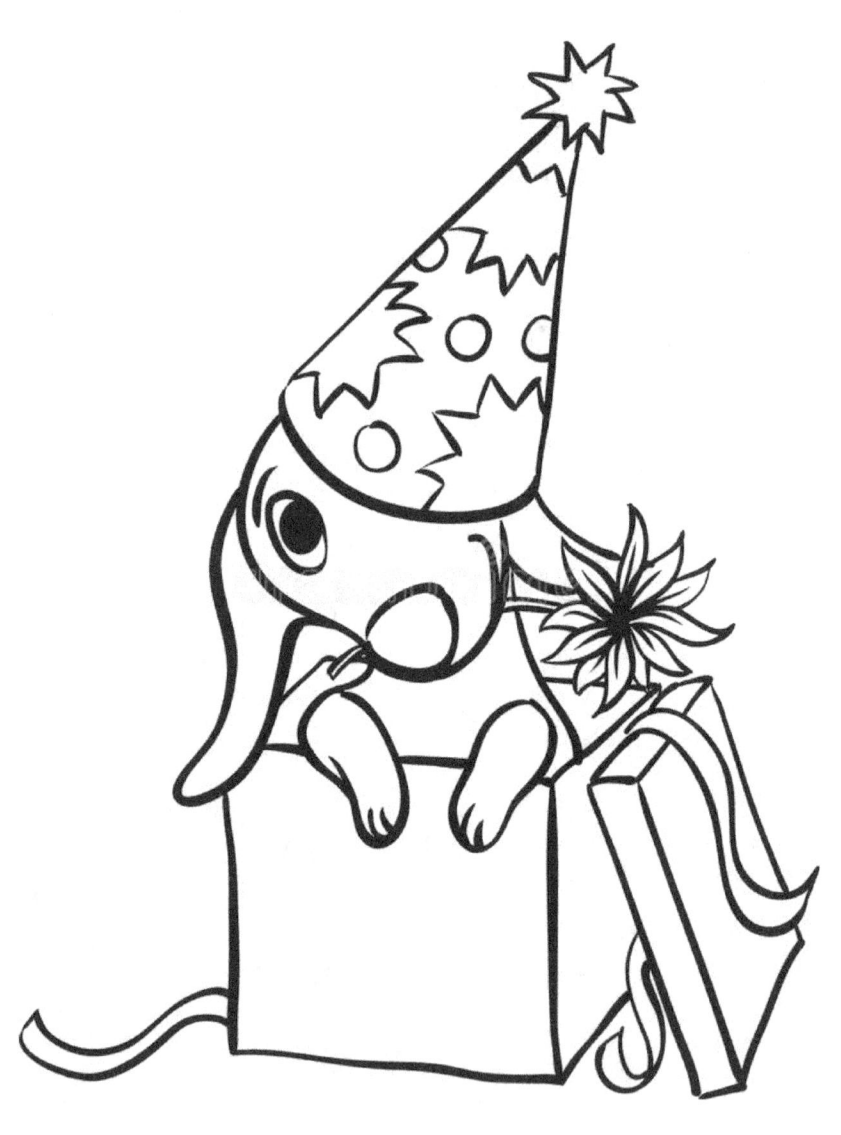

HERE IT IS, GRAB MY BONE.

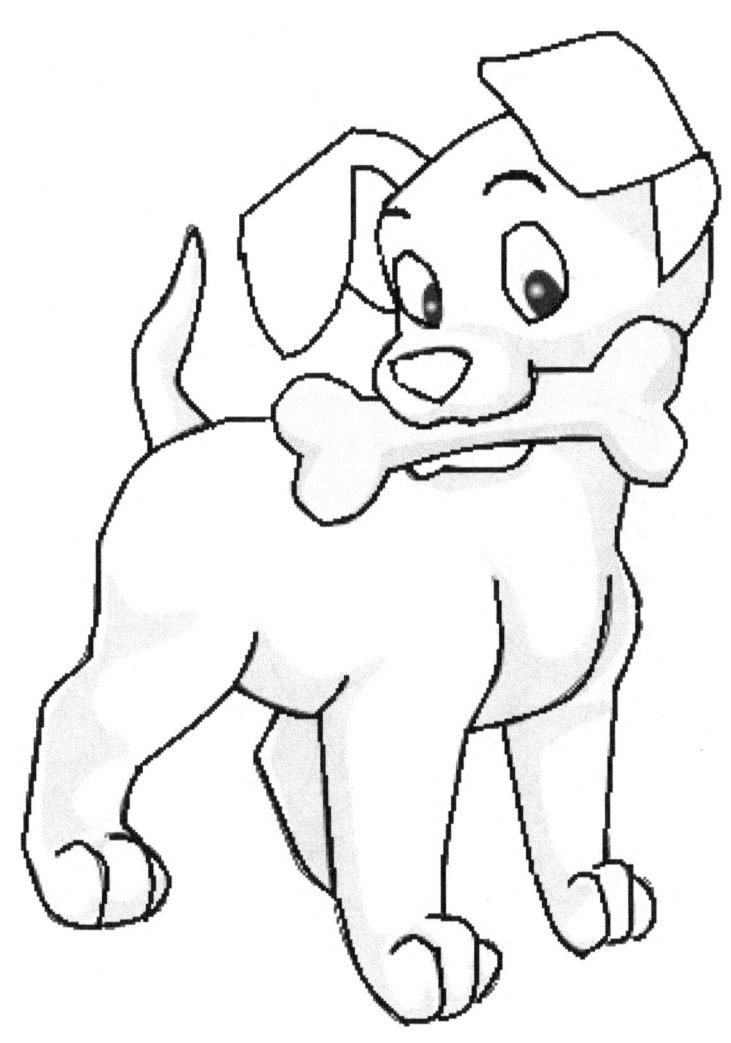

WHAT ARE YOU
LOOKING AT?

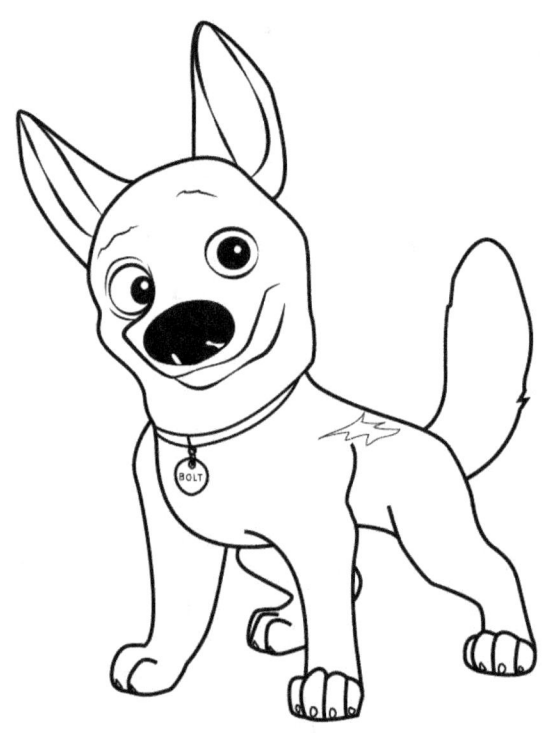

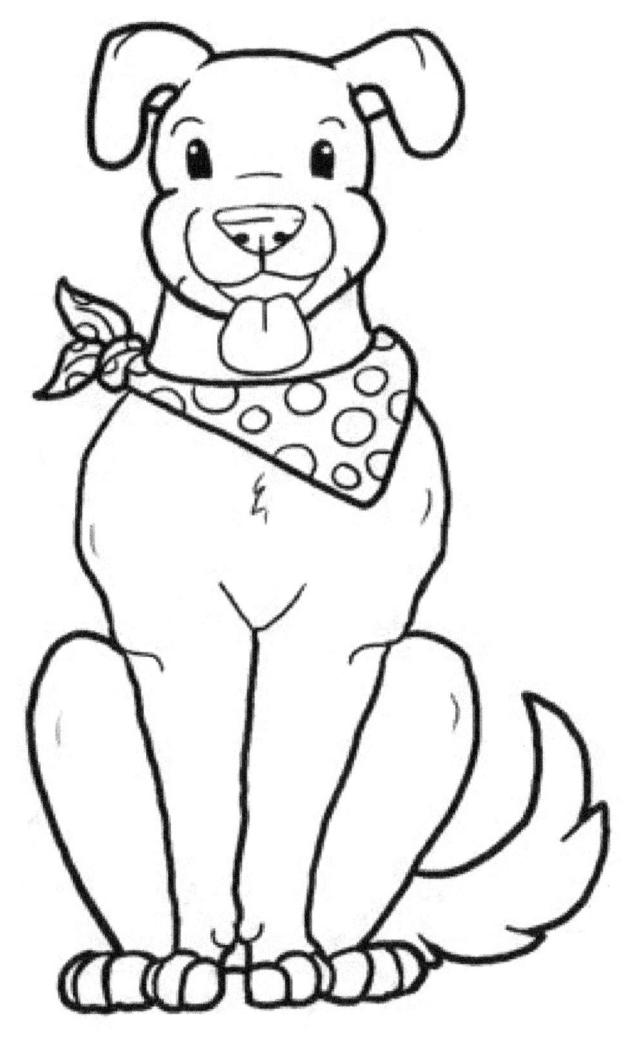

Do I look good today?

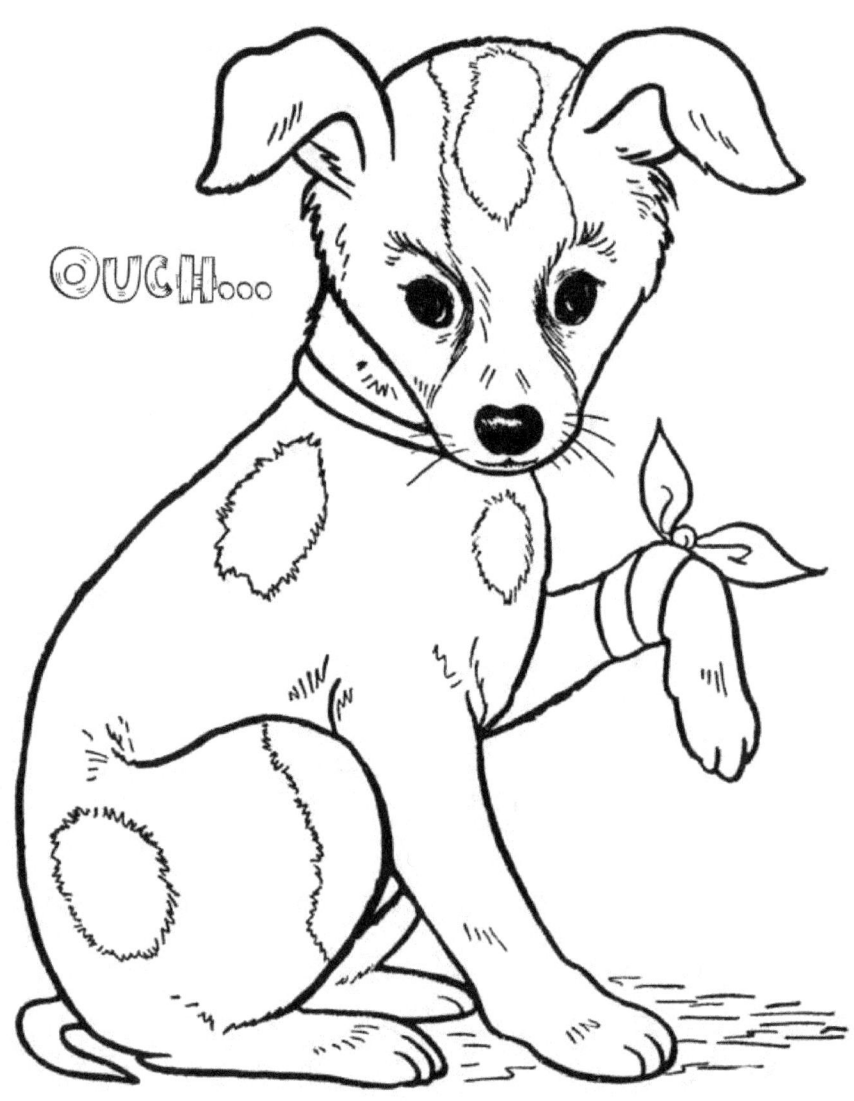

WHAT CAN I DO
FOR YOU TODAY?

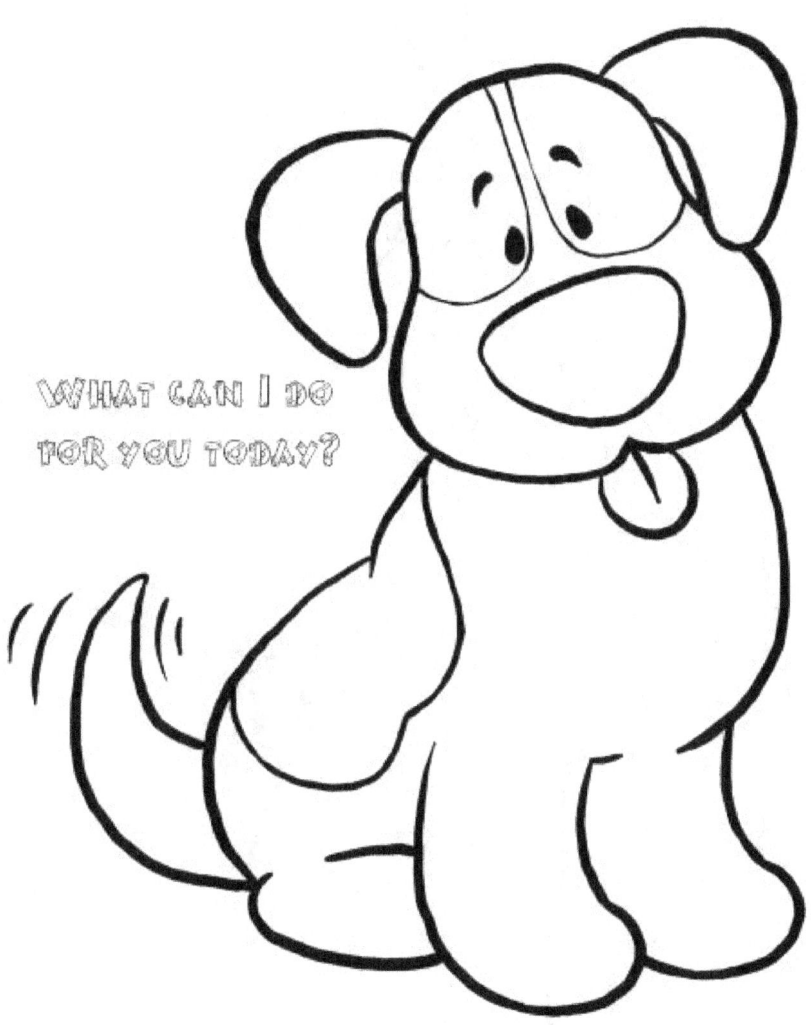

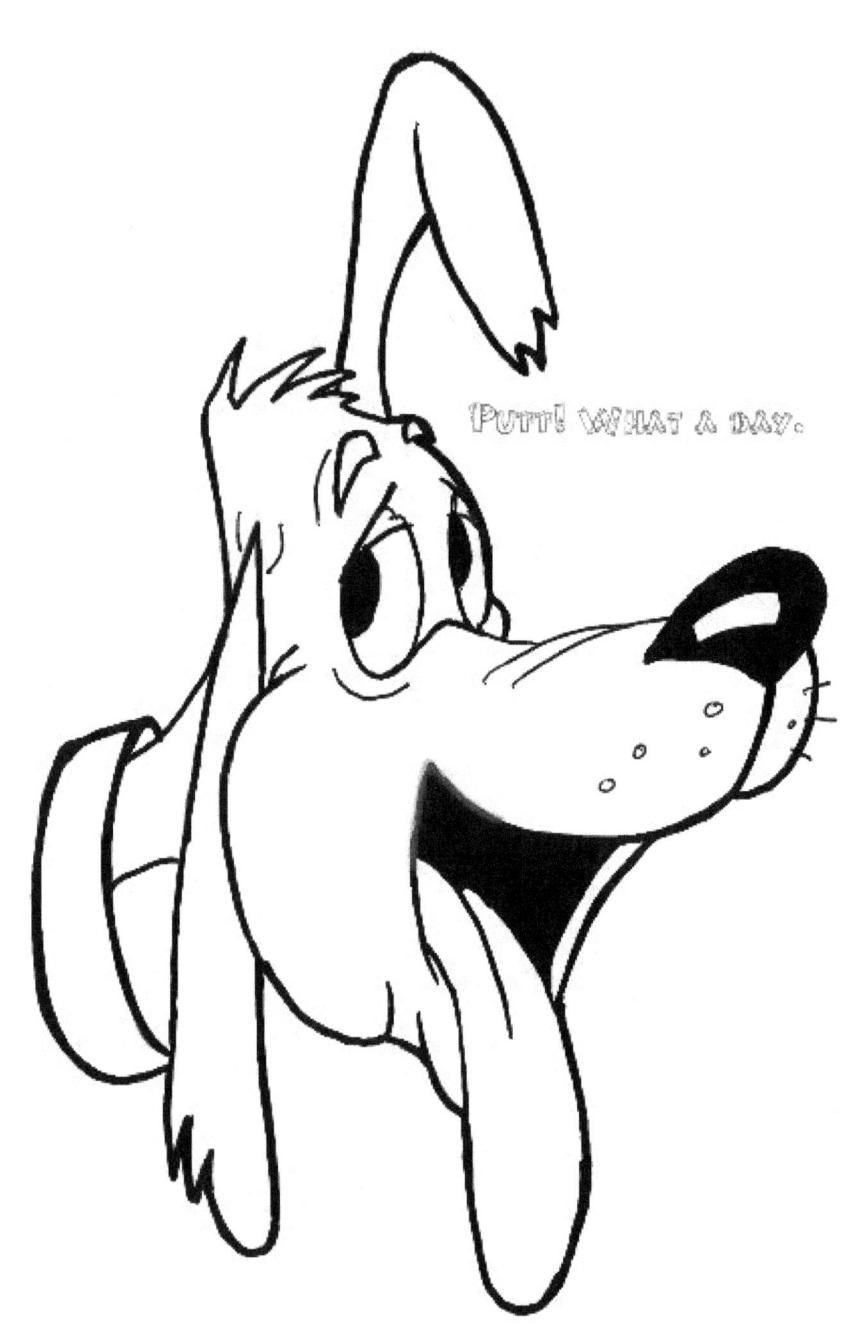

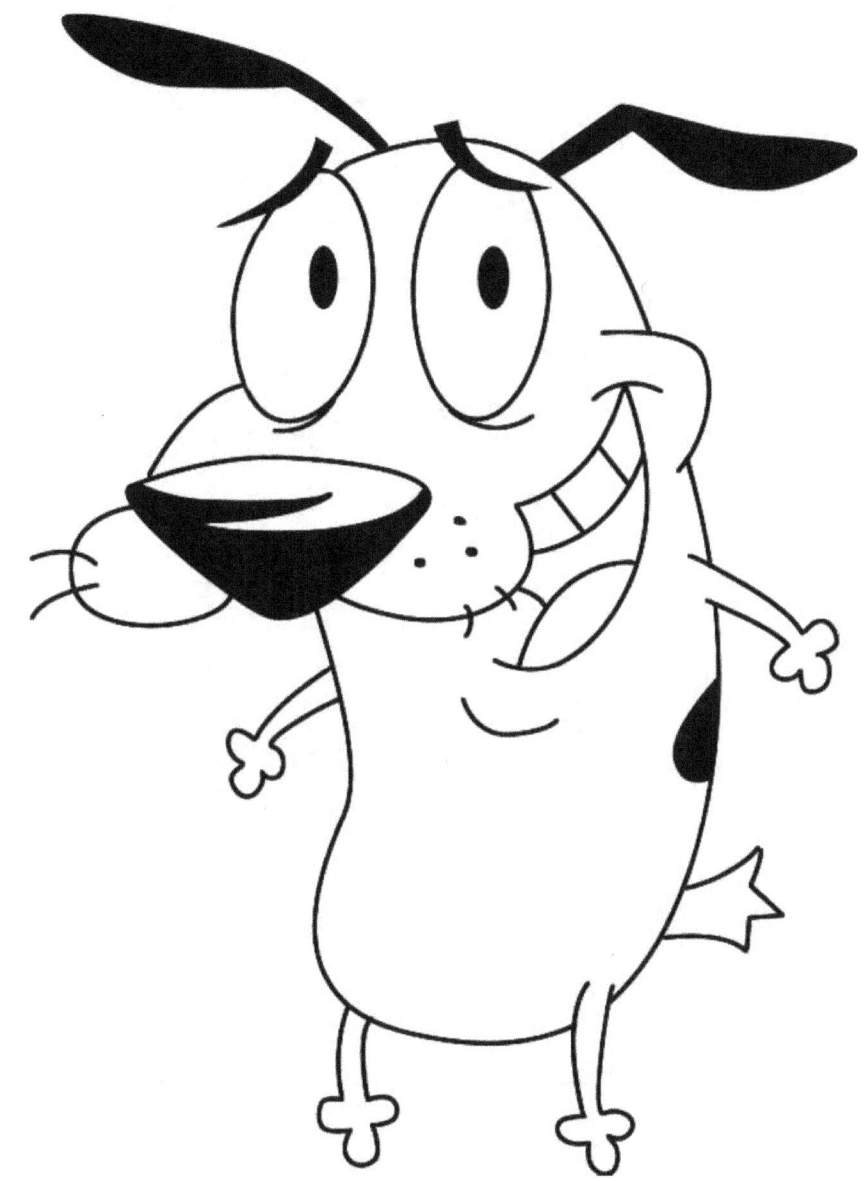

YEH! I JUST FINISHED MY POOPS!

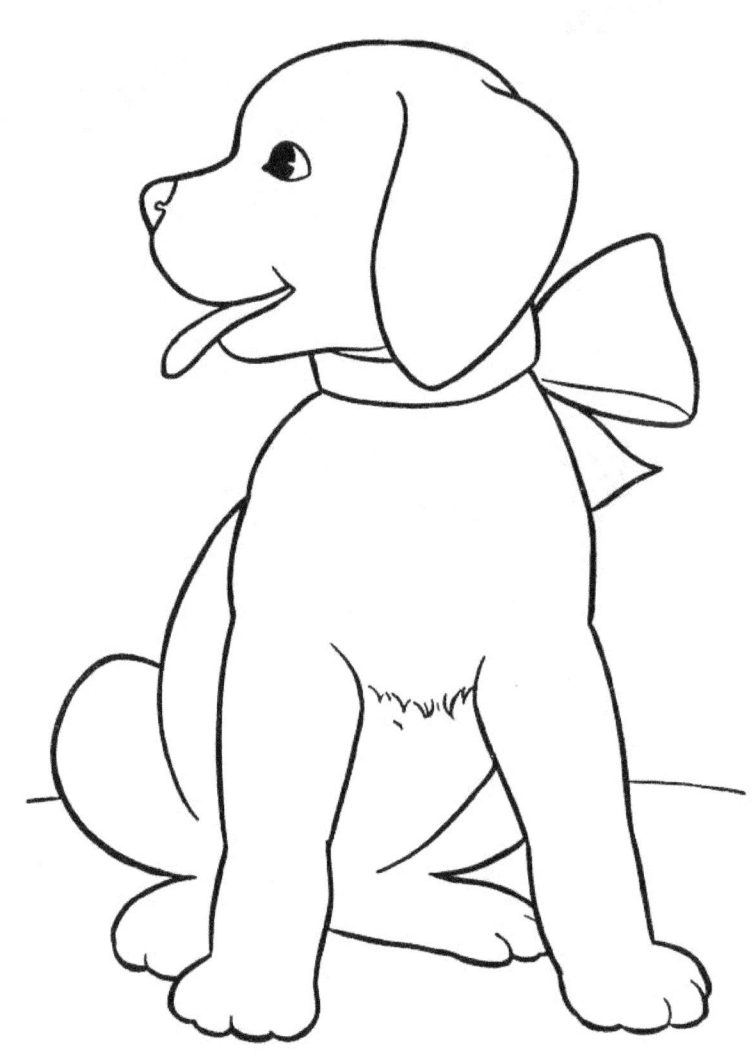

I'M FINE.

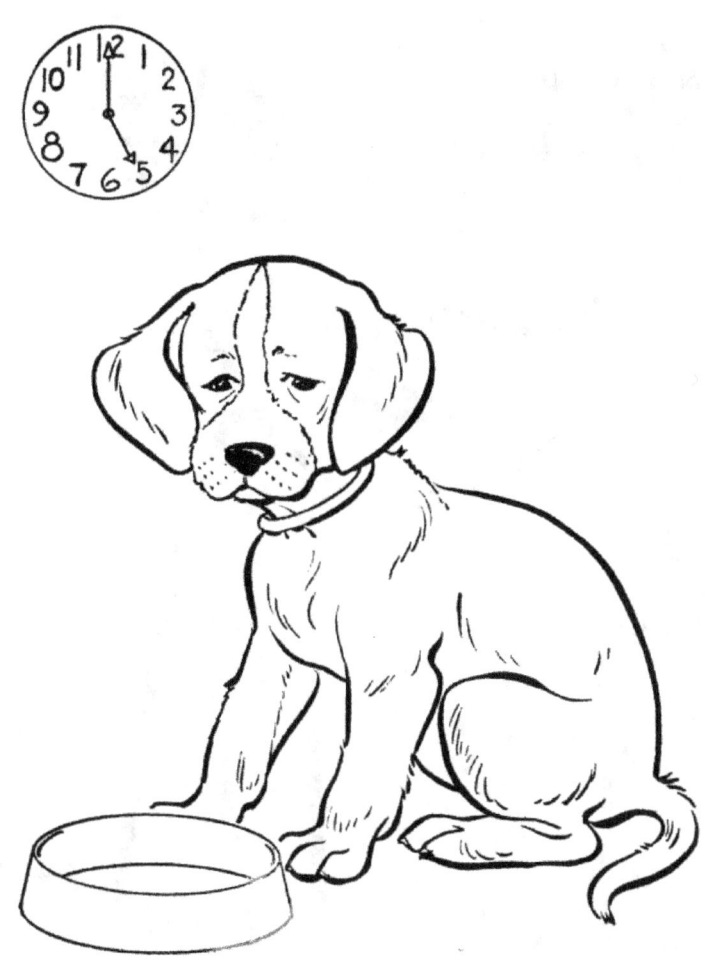

BOSS, ITS TIME.

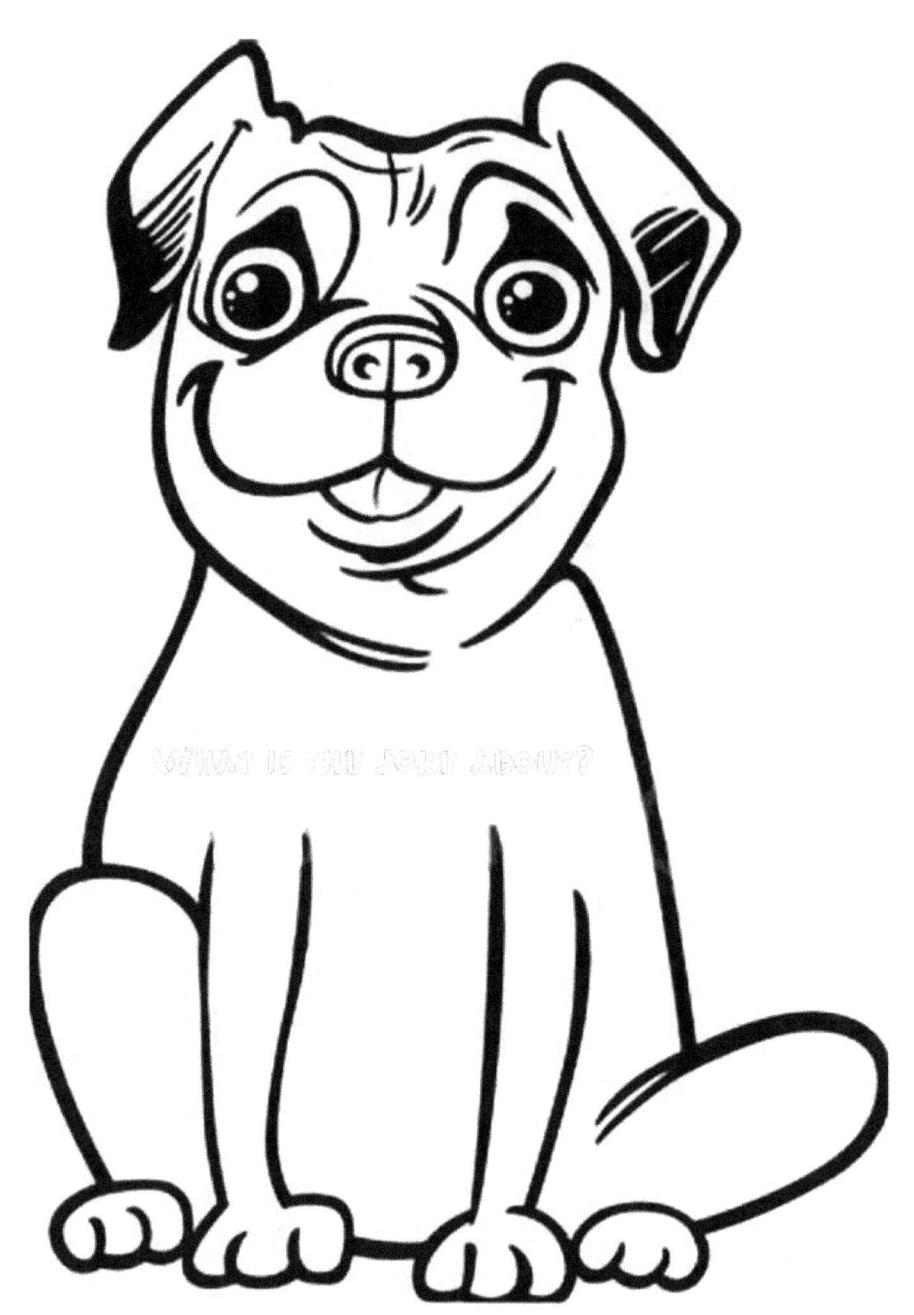

WHERE IS BOSS?

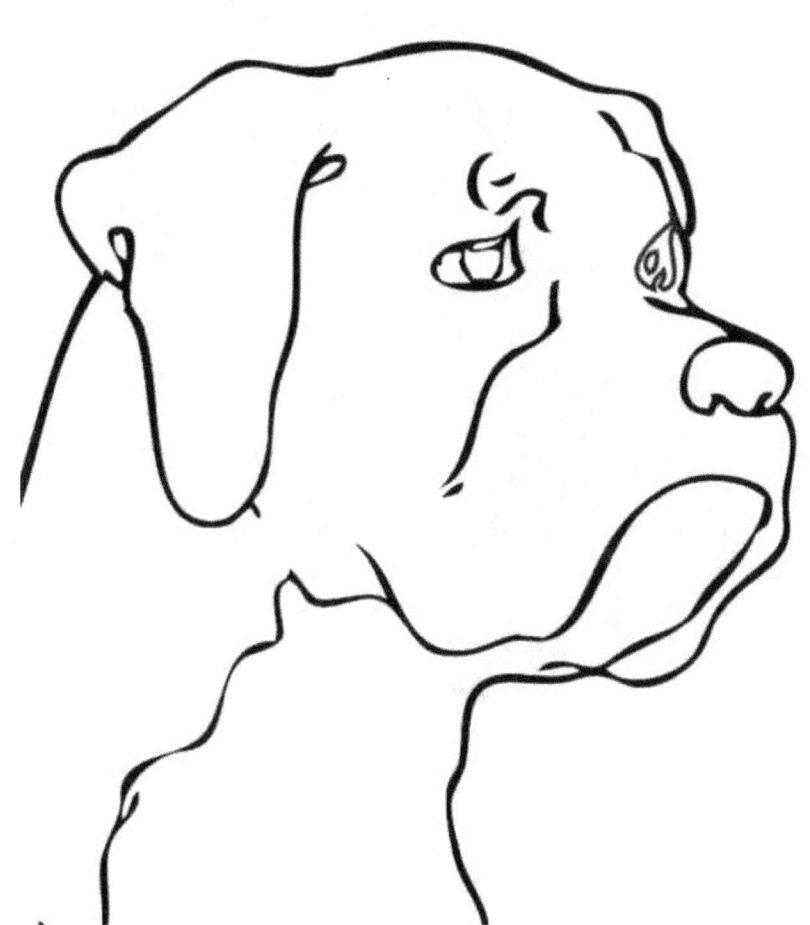

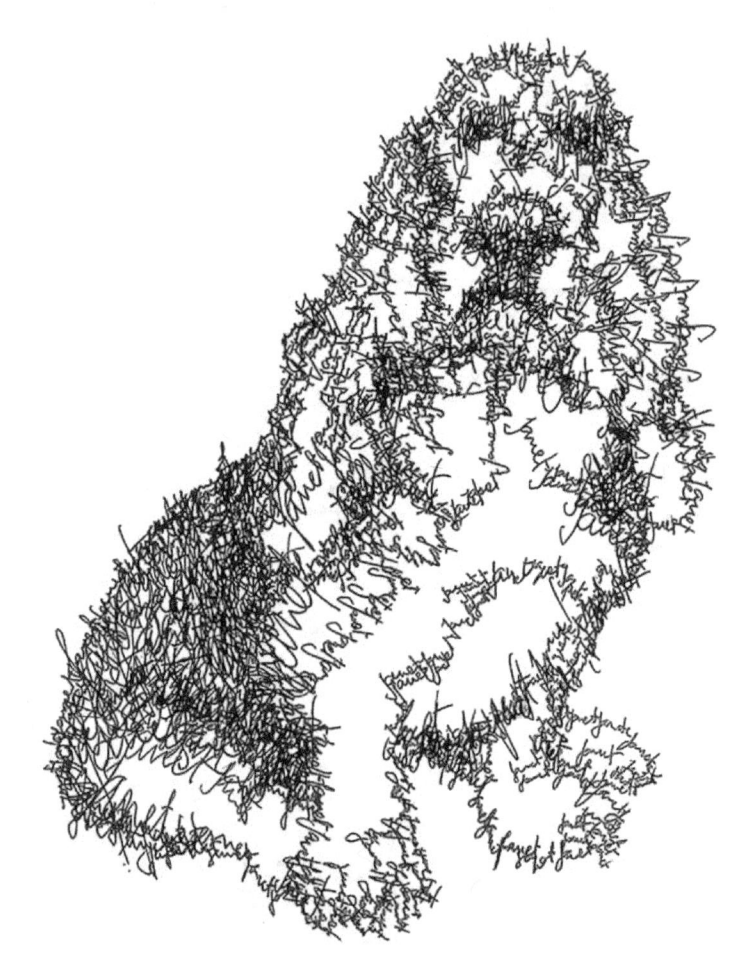

LOOKS LIKE ITS IN A MESS...

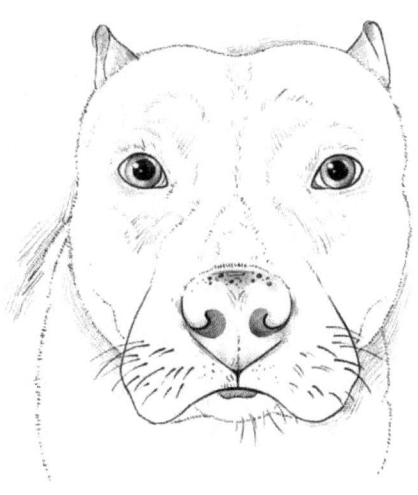

THE ROAD IS HAZY.

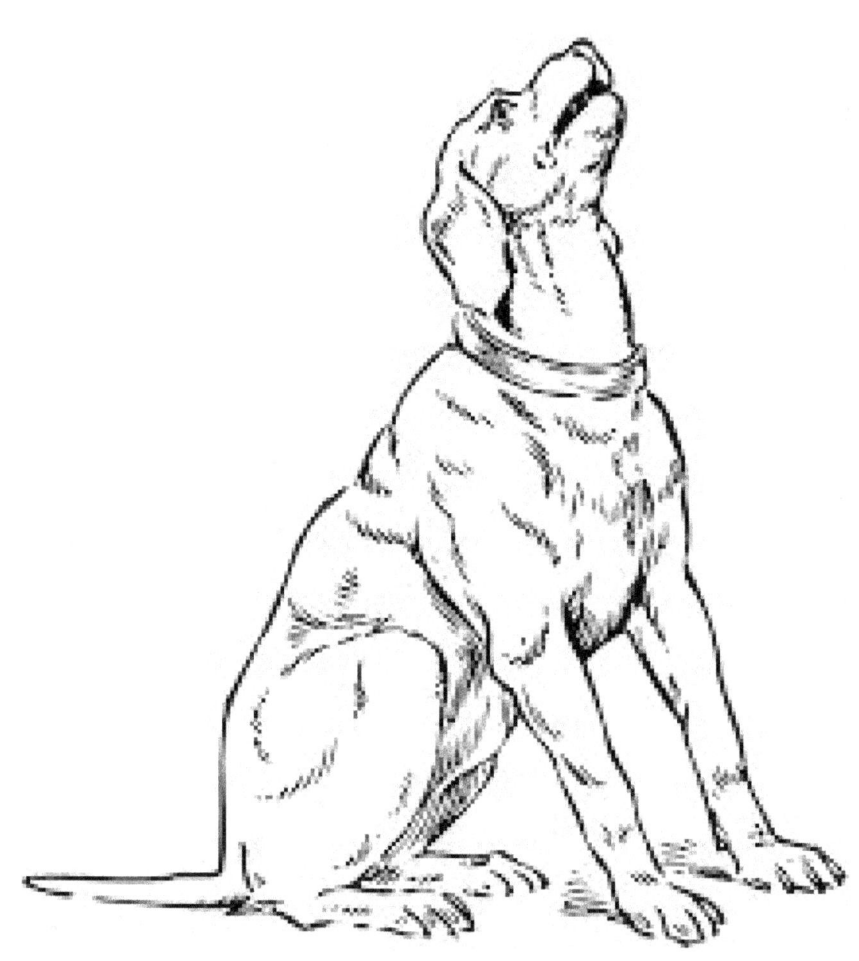

I'M SAD...

WOW, WEATHER VERY HOT.

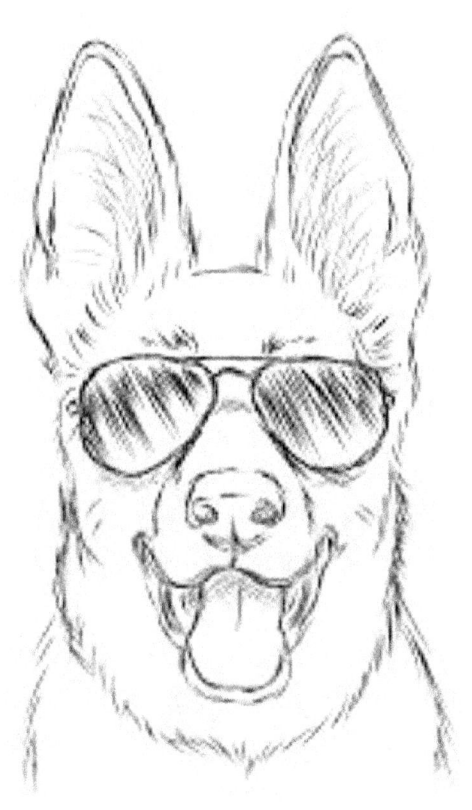

I'M SORRY, BUT...

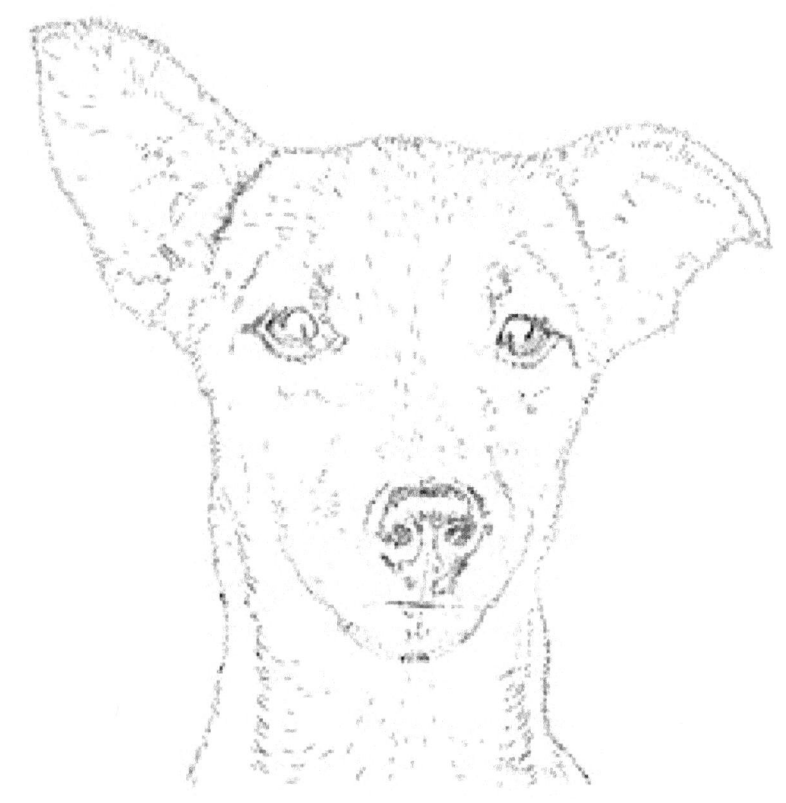

HI, HOW ARE YOU?

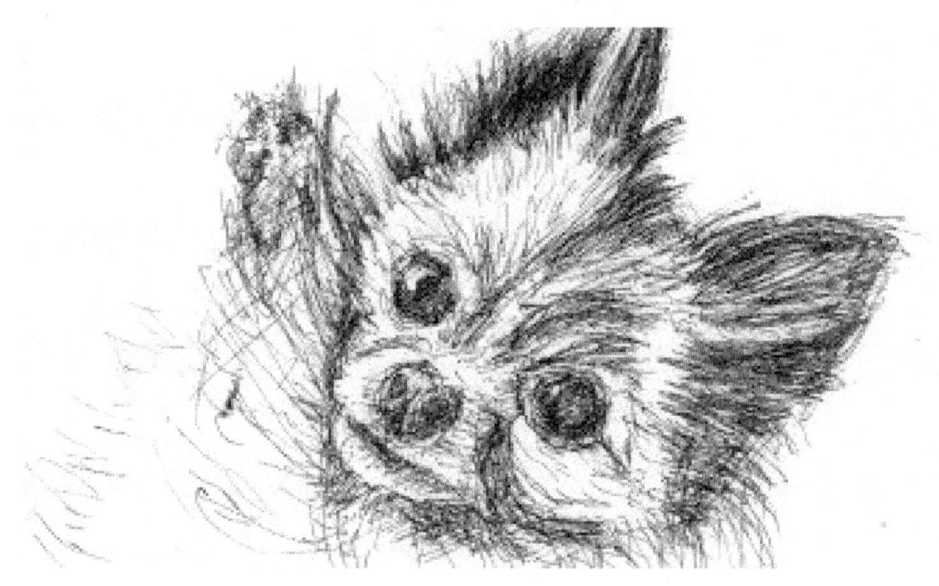

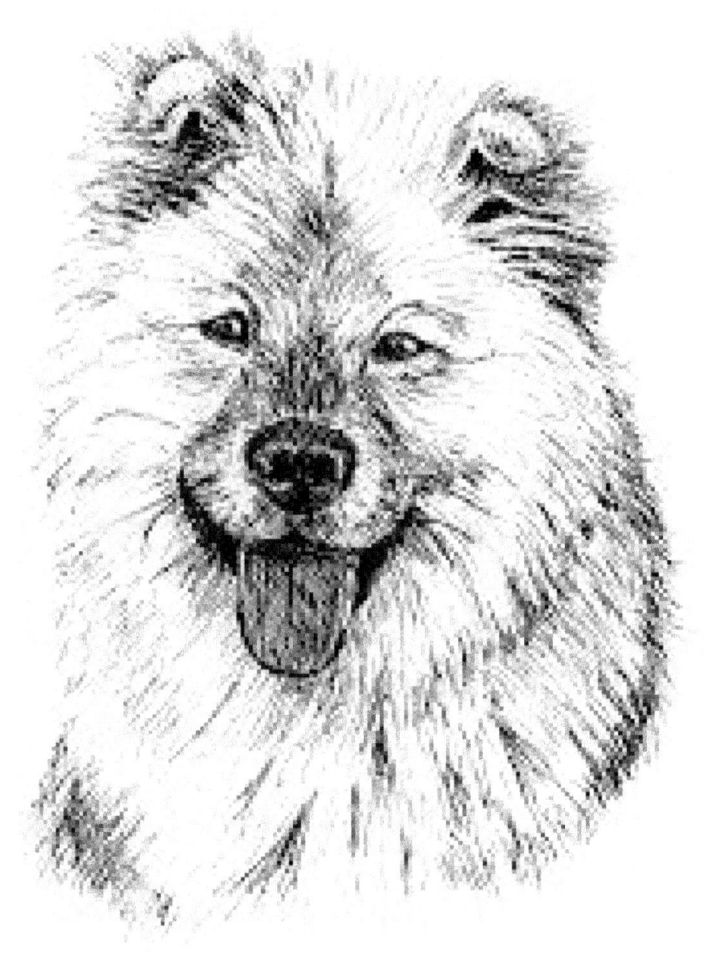

LOOK, MY BEST FRIEND IS HERE.

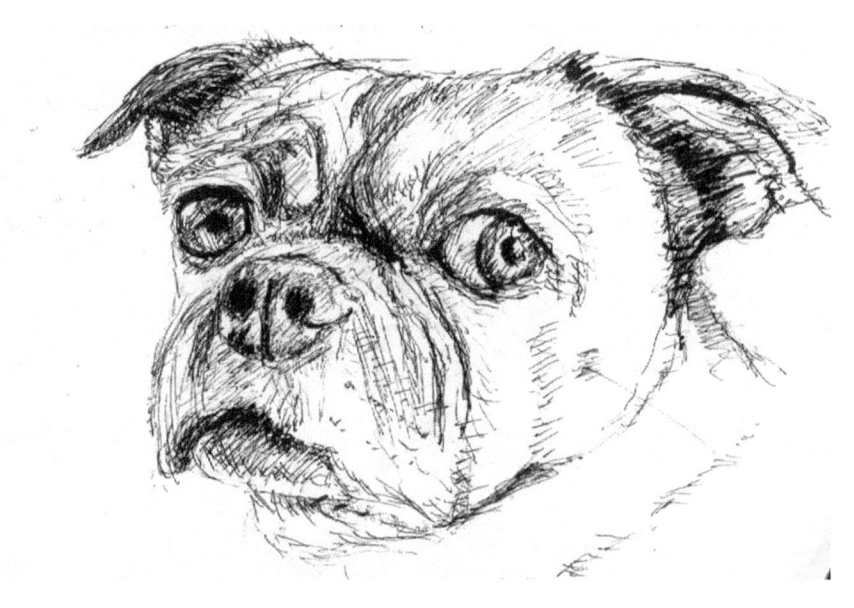

SOMETHING IS UP.

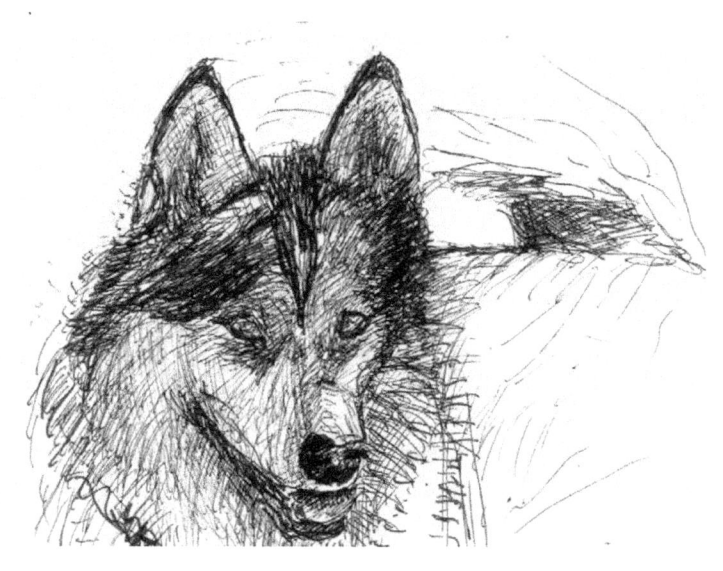

Its rather cold here...

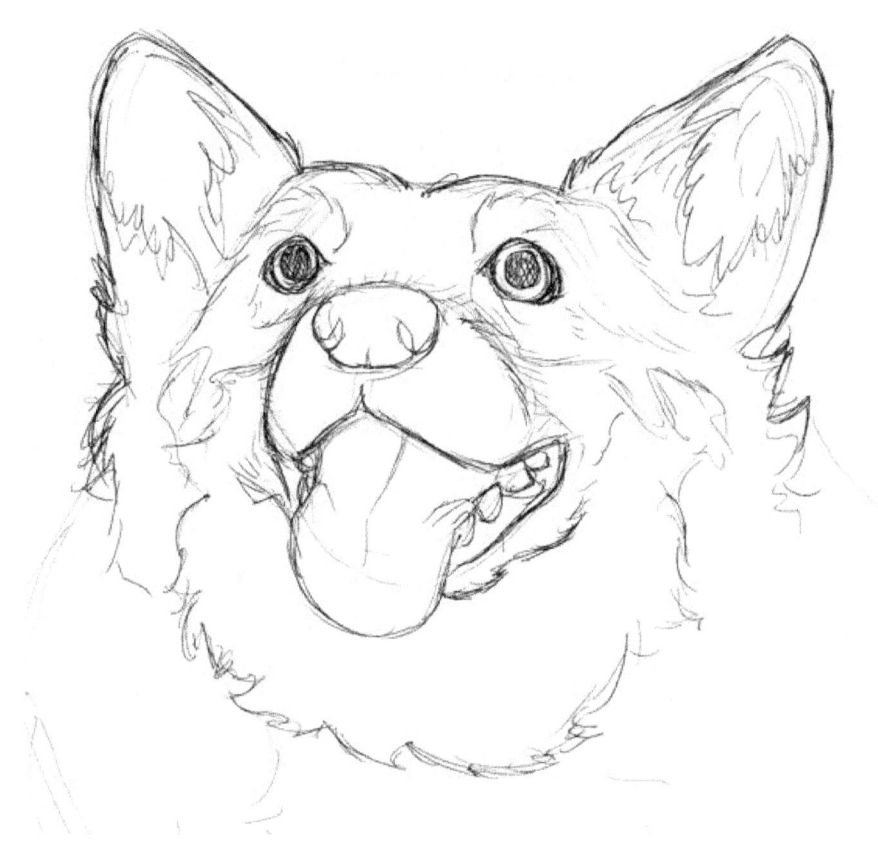

SOMEONE I LIKE IS HERE.

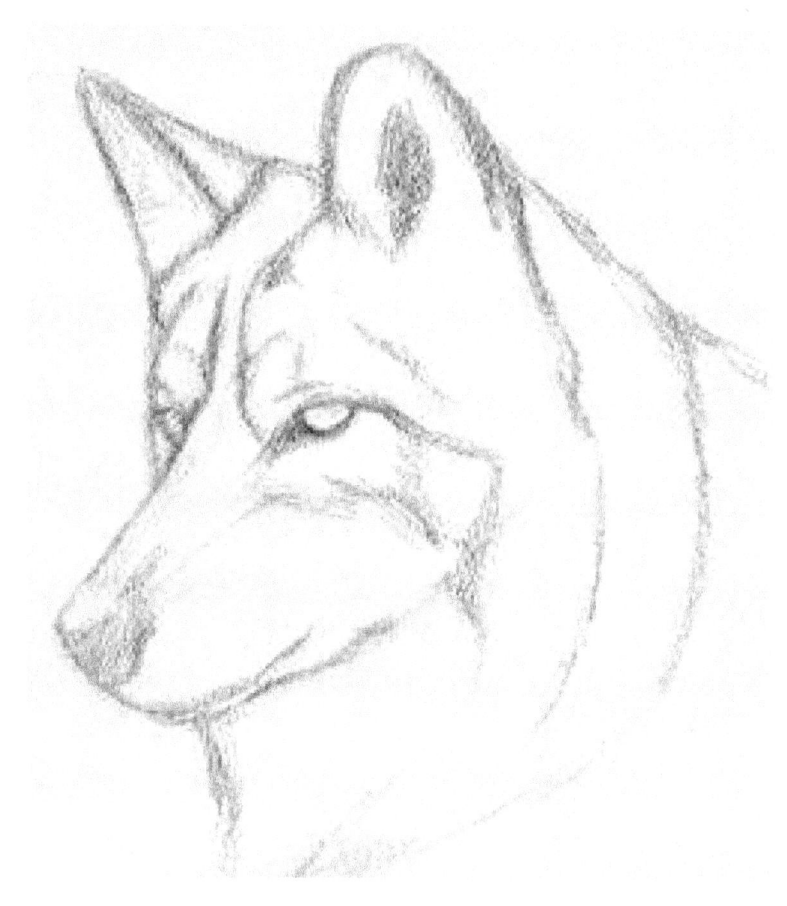

ARE YOU SLEEPY?

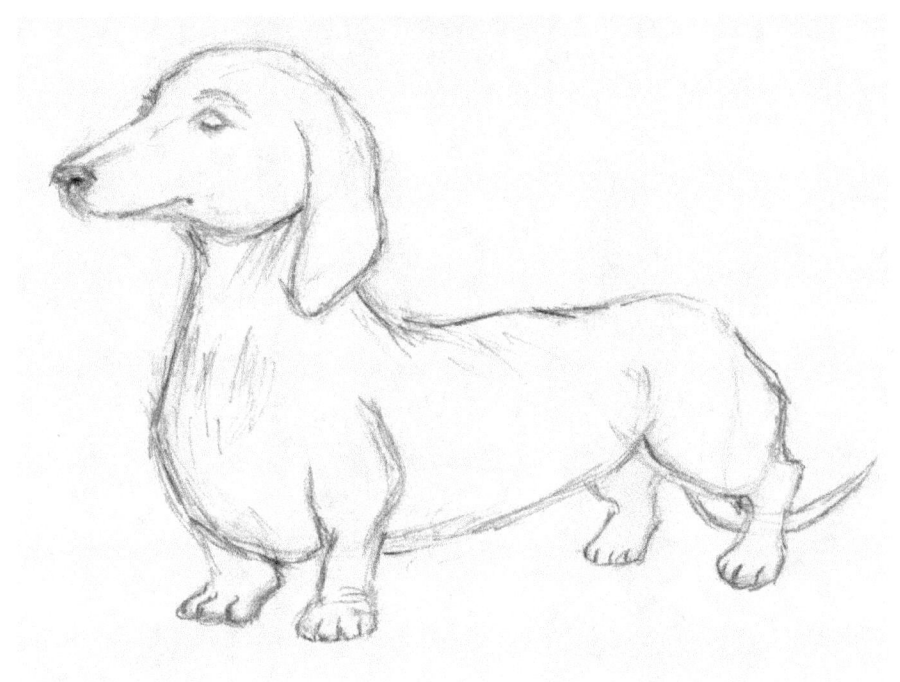

Is it you?

www.ingramcontent.com/pod-product-compliance
Lightning Source LLC
Chambersburg PA
CBHW060008230526
45472CB00008B/1995